PRINCEWILL LAGANG

Walking in Love: Christian Marriage Principles

First published by PRINCEWILL LAGANG 2023

Copyright © 2023 by Princewill Lagang

All rights reserved. No part of this publication may be reproduced, stored or transmitted in any form or by any means, electronic, mechanical, photocopying, recording, scanning, or otherwise without written permission from the publisher. It is illegal to copy this book, post it to a website, or distribute it by any other means without permission.

Princewill Lagang asserts the moral right to be identified as the author of this work.

First edition

This book was professionally typeset on Reedsy. Find out more at reedsy.com

Contents

1. Walking in Love: Christian Marriage Principles — 1
2. Trust - The Bedrock of Love — 4
3. The Power of Unity in Christian Marriage — 7
4. The Role of Prayer in Christian Marriage — 10
5. Fostering Intimacy and Emotional Connection — 13
6. Navigating Conflict with Love and Grace — 16
7. Honoring Your Covenant - Perseverance and Renewal — 18
8. Building a Legacy of Love — 21
9. Supporting Each Other's Spiritual Growth — 24
10. Cherishing and Celebrating Your Love — 26
11. The Gift of Forgiveness — 28
12. The Joy of Serving Together — 30

1

Walking in Love: Christian Marriage Principles

Introduction

Marriage is often described as a journey, a sacred covenant, and a lifelong commitment. It is a union where two individuals embark on a shared path, facing challenges and celebrating joys together. In this journey, love is the compass that guides and sustains the marriage. As the Apostle Paul eloquently wrote in 1 Corinthians 13:4-7, "Love is patient, love is kind. It does not envy, it does not boast, it is not proud. It does not dishonor others, it is not self-seeking, it is not easily angered, it keeps no record of wrongs. Love does not delight in evil but rejoices with the truth. It always protects, always trusts, always hopes, always perseveres."

In this book, we will delve into the essence of Christian marriage principles, centered on the foundation of love. Whether you are newlyweds, in the midst of a thriving marriage, or facing challenges in your relationship, the principles of Christian marriage can guide you to walk in love, experience lasting joy, and grow closer to God and each other.

Chapter 1: Love as the Cornerstone

In the opening chapter of our exploration into Christian marriage principles, we begin at the very heart of it all – love. Love is not merely a feeling but a choice, a commitment, and a way of life. Christian marriage is built on the belief that God is love, and as His children, we are called to emulate His love in our relationships.

Section 1: The Biblical Foundation of Love

To understand love in the context of Christian marriage, we must turn to the Bible, where we find numerous passages that expound on the nature of love. The aforementioned passage from 1 Corinthians 13 is one of the most quoted scriptures when it comes to love, but there are many others like John 3:16, which reminds us of the profound nature of God's love.

Section 2: Agape Love

In Christian theology, love is often categorized into different types, with "agape" being the highest form of love. Agape love is unconditional, sacrificial, and selfless. It is the love that God has for His creation, and it's the love that Christians are called to have for one another in marriage and in all relationships. We will explore what it means to practice agape love in the context of a Christian marriage.

Section 3: Love as a Choice

Love is not solely a fleeting emotion but a deliberate choice. In Christian marriage, love is a commitment to care for, honor, and cherish one's spouse, even in the face of challenges. We will discuss how making this choice daily can transform a marriage and create a strong foundation for a lifelong journey together.

Section 4: The Role of Love in Conflict Resolution

No marriage is without its challenges, and conflicts are inevitable. In this section, we will discuss how love can be the guiding light in resolving disagreements and maintaining harmony. We will explore the concept of "turning the other cheek" and how it can be applied within the marriage context.

Section 5: Growing in Love Together

Love is not static; it's dynamic and should continuously grow and deepen. We will conclude this chapter by discussing how couples can foster and nurture love throughout their marriage journey. This includes the importance of communication, forgiveness, and spiritual growth as a couple.

Conclusion

In this opening chapter, we have laid the foundation for our exploration of Christian marriage principles. Love, as the cornerstone of this journey, will be our constant companion as we delve into topics such as trust, communication, intimacy, and more. With the biblical foundation of love as our guide, we will navigate the path of Christian marriage, seeking to honor God, love our spouse, and experience the fullness of this sacred covenant.

2

Trust - The Bedrock of Love

In our exploration of Christian marriage principles, we move from the foundation of love to another essential element that upholds the sacred bond between husband and wife: trust. Trust is the bedrock upon which a successful Christian marriage is built. Without trust, the love that we discussed in the previous chapter remains fragile and susceptible to erosion. This chapter will delve into the significance of trust in Christian marriage and how to cultivate and maintain it.

Section 1: The Biblical Perspective on Trust

In Christian marriage, trust is more than just a psychological and emotional bond; it is deeply rooted in the biblical principles of faith and fidelity. We will explore passages from the Bible that highlight the importance of trust in our relationship with God and in our earthly relationships, including marriage.

Section 2: Trusting in God's Plan

Trust in marriage begins with trust in God's plan for your union. Understanding that God brought you together for a purpose and that He is a part of your marriage journey can provide a strong foundation for trust between spouses. We will discuss how faith in God's sovereignty can alleviate anxiety and strengthen the bond between husband and wife.

Section 3: Open and Honest Communication

Effective communication is the vehicle through which trust is built and maintained. In this section, we will explore the role of open and honest communication in nurturing trust within a Christian marriage. We will discuss the importance of active listening, vulnerability, and transparency.

Section 4: Trust and Forgiveness

Forgiveness is a key component of trust in a Christian marriage. Just as God forgives our sins, we are called to forgive each other in marriage. We will examine how the practice of forgiveness can mend trust when it's been broken and strengthen it when it's intact.

Section 5: Boundaries and Accountability

Setting healthy boundaries and practicing accountability within a marriage are vital aspects of trust. We will discuss the importance of respecting each other's boundaries while being accountable to one another. This creates a safe and secure environment where trust can thrive.

Section 6: Rebuilding Trust

Sometimes trust can be damaged, and rebuilding it can be a challenging process. This section will provide guidance on how to navigate the journey of rebuilding trust, emphasizing the role of repentance, patience, and commitment in the restoration of a trusting relationship.

Conclusion

Trust is the invisible thread that weaves the fabric of a Christian marriage. It is a reflection of the trust we place in God and the trust we place in each other. This chapter has explored the biblical foundation of trust, the importance of trust in God's plan, and practical ways to build and rebuild trust within a marriage. As you continue your journey in Christian marriage, remember that trust is not only a gift you give to your spouse but a testament to your faith in God's design for your union. In the chapters to come, we will explore more principles that will help you walk in love and faith in your Christian marriage.

3

The Power of Unity in Christian Marriage

In Christian marriage, unity is a force that transcends the mere union of two individuals. It is a spiritual bond that reflects the divine unity of Christ with His Church. This chapter explores the significance of unity within a Christian marriage, its biblical foundations, and how it can be harnessed to strengthen the love shared by husband and wife.

Section 1: The Biblical Model of Unity

The Bible often uses the imagery of marriage to describe the relationship between Christ and the Church. This section will delve into passages that emphasize the unity between Christ and the Church, highlighting how it serves as a model for the unity between spouses in Christian marriage.

Section 2: The Threefold Cord

Ecclesiastes 4:12 tells us that "a cord of three strands is not quickly broken." In a Christian marriage, the three strands symbolize God, husband, and wife. We will explore how inviting God into your marriage as the third strand can reinforce unity and provide a firm foundation for your relationship.

Section 3: Shared Values and Vision

Unity is often born from shared values and a common vision. We will discuss the importance of aligning your core beliefs and long-term goals within your marriage, and how doing so can strengthen the unity between spouses.

Section 4: Roles and Responsibilities

In Christian marriage, unity doesn't imply uniformity. Each spouse has unique roles and responsibilities within the marriage, as outlined in the Bible. This section will explore how understanding and fulfilling these roles can enhance the unity of your marriage while honoring the individuality of each partner.

Section 5: Conflict Resolution and Reconciliation

Even in the most harmonious marriages, conflicts may arise. We will discuss how unity can guide the process of conflict resolution and reconciliation within a Christian marriage, emphasizing the importance of approaching disputes with love, understanding, and a commitment to maintaining unity.

Section 6: Celebrating Milestones Together

To maintain unity, it's essential to celebrate the milestones and achievements in your marriage. This section will discuss the importance of cherishing these moments, whether they're small victories or major accomplishments, as a way of nurturing unity and mutual support.

Conclusion

Unity in a Christian marriage is not merely a pleasant aspiration but a powerful and transformative force. It's a reflection of the unity between Christ and the Church, and it can fortify your love, faith, and commitment to one another. In this chapter, we've explored the biblical model of unity, the significance of inviting God into your marriage, the importance of shared values and vision, roles and responsibilities, and navigating conflict and celebrating together. As you continue your journey in Christian marriage, remember that unity is a gift that binds your love and faith together, allowing you to walk hand in hand in the light of God's love.

4

The Role of Prayer in Christian Marriage

Prayer is a powerful and intimate means of communication with God, and it holds a special place within Christian marriage. In this chapter, we will explore the significance of prayer in strengthening the bond between husband and wife, deepening their faith, and nurturing a love that is rooted in God.

Section 1: The Biblical Foundation of Prayer

The Bible is replete with passages that emphasize the importance of prayer in the lives of Christians. In this section, we will explore scriptures that highlight the value of prayer in seeking God's guidance, finding solace in difficult times, and maintaining a relationship with the divine.

Section 2: Individual and Shared Prayer Life

In Christian marriage, individual and shared prayer lives are both crucial. We will discuss the significance of personal prayer, where each spouse can draw closer to God individually. Additionally, we will explore the benefits of shared prayer, where husband and wife come together in supplication, thanksgiving, and intercession.

Section 3: Praying for Your Spouse

Praying for your spouse is a powerful act of love and devotion. We will delve into how specific and intentional prayers for your partner can strengthen your connection, support one another's growth, and deepen your commitment to walking in love together.

Section 4: Praying Through Challenges and Celebrations

Prayer isn't just for difficult times; it's also a vital component of celebrating the joys and blessings in your marriage. We will discuss how to bring both your challenges and celebrations to God through prayer, seeking His wisdom, guidance, and thanksgiving.

Section 5: Cultivating Spiritual Intimacy

Prayer is a means of cultivating spiritual intimacy in your marriage. We will explore how sharing your spiritual journey, fears, hopes, and dreams through prayer can draw you closer to one another and to God.

Section 6: Aligning Your Marriage with God's Will

One of the most profound aspects of prayer is seeking God's will for your marriage. We will discuss how prayer can be used to discern God's plan for your life together, seeking His guidance in major decisions, and finding the path that aligns with His divine purpose.

Conclusion

Prayer is a lifeline for Christian marriages, connecting spouses to each other and to God. It provides a means to draw upon God's wisdom, strength, and love in times of joy and challenge. In this chapter, we've explored the biblical foundation of prayer, the significance of individual and shared prayer life, praying for your spouse, bringing your challenges and celebrations to God, cultivating spiritual intimacy, and aligning your marriage with God's will through prayer. As you continue your journey in Christian marriage, remember that prayer is a powerful tool for nurturing love, faith, and unity, providing you with the spiritual resources to walk hand in hand with God.

5

Fostering Intimacy and Emotional Connection

Intimacy is a foundational component of a thriving Christian marriage. This chapter explores the various dimensions of intimacy within the context of a Christian relationship and provides guidance on how to cultivate and maintain emotional closeness.

Section 1: The Biblical Perspective on Intimacy

The Bible not only acknowledges the physical aspect of intimacy in marriage but also emphasizes the importance of emotional and spiritual closeness between spouses. In this section, we will explore biblical passages that highlight the significance of intimacy within Christian marriage.

Section 2: Emotional Intimacy

Emotional intimacy involves a deep connection and vulnerability in sharing thoughts, feelings, and experiences. We will discuss how to foster emotional intimacy by actively listening, supporting, and understanding each other on a profound level.

Section 3: Spiritual Intimacy

Spiritual intimacy is the shared connection between a husband and wife in their faith journey. We will delve into how couples can grow spiritually together, praying together, studying the Bible, and supporting each other's spiritual growth.

Section 4: Physical Intimacy

While physical intimacy is often a focus in discussions about marriage, it's essential to approach it with a foundation of love, trust, and consent. We will explore how physical intimacy can be a beautiful expression of love and unity when approached with mutual respect and understanding.

Section 5: Maintaining Intimacy Amidst Life's Challenges

Life's challenges can put a strain on intimacy, but they can also be opportunities for growth. This section will provide guidance on maintaining emotional, spiritual, and physical intimacy during difficult times, emphasizing the importance of support and communication.

Section 6: Date Nights and Quality Time

Regularly spending quality time together is an effective way to foster intimacy. We will discuss the importance of date nights and dedicated moments for connecting, conversing, and rekindling the love and intimacy in your marriage.

Conclusion

Intimacy is the soul of a Christian marriage, uniting love, trust, and spiritual connection. It is more than physical closeness; it is an all-encompassing bond that celebrates your relationship's emotional, spiritual, and physical aspects.

In this chapter, we've explored the biblical perspective on intimacy, emotional intimacy, spiritual intimacy, physical intimacy, maintaining intimacy during challenges, and the importance of quality time together. As you continue your journey in Christian marriage, remember that fostering intimacy is a continuous process that can deepen your love and faith while strengthening the unity of your relationship.

6

Navigating Conflict with Love and Grace

Conflict is an inevitable part of any marriage, but how couples approach and resolve it can make all the difference. In this chapter, we will explore the principles of resolving conflicts with love, grace, and a Christian perspective, strengthening the bond between husband and wife in the process.

Section 1: The Purpose of Conflict

Conflict is not necessarily a sign of a troubled marriage. It can serve as an opportunity for growth, understanding, and increased intimacy. In this section, we will discuss the purpose of conflict and how it can be used to strengthen a Christian marriage.

Section 2: Active Listening and Empathy

Effective conflict resolution begins with active listening and empathy. We will explore the importance of genuinely hearing your spouse's perspective, showing empathy, and seeking to understand their feelings and needs.

Section 3: A Biblical Approach to Conflict

The Bible provides guidance on how to handle disagreements with love and grace. We will delve into biblical principles for conflict resolution, including forgiveness, humility, and seeking God's wisdom in resolving disputes.

Section 4: Humility and Self-Examination

In conflicts, humility is a vital virtue. We will discuss the significance of humility and self-examination, acknowledging our own shortcomings and being willing to make amends when necessary.

Section 5: Seeking Resolution and Reconciliation

Conflict resolution is about seeking a positive outcome and reconciliation. We will explore practical strategies for finding common ground, compromising, and restoring harmony after a conflict.

Section 6: The Role of Prayer in Conflict Resolution

Prayer is a powerful tool in navigating conflicts. We will discuss how prayer can bring a sense of peace, wisdom, and perspective to the conflict resolution process, enabling couples to seek God's guidance together.

Conclusion

Conflict is an inevitable part of any relationship, but in a Christian marriage, it can be a transformative and strengthening force. Navigating conflict with love and grace, guided by biblical principles, allows couples to grow in their faith, love, and unity. In this chapter, we've explored the purpose of conflict, active listening, a biblical approach to conflict, humility, seeking resolution, and the role of prayer in conflict resolution. As you continue your journey in Christian marriage, remember that conflicts can be opportunities for growth and deeper connection, provided they are approached with love and grace, guided by your faith in God and your love for one another.

7

Honoring Your Covenant - Perseverance and Renewal

A Christian marriage is not only a commitment made on the wedding day but a continuous journey of faith, love, and perseverance. In this chapter, we will explore the importance of honoring the covenant you've made, embracing perseverance, and renewing your commitment to each other and to God.

Section 1: The Sacredness of the Marriage Covenant

The marriage covenant is a sacred promise before God, and it's intended to be upheld for a lifetime. We will discuss the significance of this covenant and how it reflects the relationship between Christ and His Church.

Section 2: The Challenges of a Lifelong Commitment

The journey of a Christian marriage is not without challenges. We will explore the common obstacles couples may face, such as communication issues, external pressures, and personal growth, and how to navigate them while staying true to your covenant.

Section 3: Perseverance Through Tough Times

Perseverance is a fundamental principle in Christian marriage. We will discuss how to endure through difficult seasons, drawing strength from your faith, love, and the support of your spouse, family, and community.

Section 4: Renewal of Vows and Commitment

Renewing your vows can be a powerful way to reaffirm your commitment to each other and to God. We will explore the significance of vow renewal ceremonies and how they can strengthen your bond and rekindle your love.

Section 5: Keeping God at the Center

Maintaining a strong and lasting marriage necessitates keeping God at the center of your relationship. We will discuss the importance of maintaining a vibrant spiritual life individually and as a couple, drawing strength and guidance from your faith.

Section 6: Love, Faith, and the Journey Forward

The journey of a Christian marriage is a testament to the enduring power of love and faith. We will conclude this chapter by reflecting on how love, faith, and a commitment to honoring your covenant can guide your marriage journey and lead to a fulfilling and lasting partnership.

Conclusion

A Christian marriage is a sacred covenant that requires continuous commitment, perseverance, and renewal. In this chapter, we've explored the significance of the marriage covenant, the challenges of lifelong commitment, perseverance through tough times, the renewal of vows and commitment, keeping God at the center, and the enduring power of love and faith. As you continue your journey in Christian marriage, remember that the covenant you've made is a testament to your love and faith, and by honoring it, you not only strengthen your marriage but also reflect the enduring love of Christ for His Church.

8

Building a Legacy of Love

A Christian marriage is not only a commitment between two individuals; it is also a legacy that impacts future generations. In this chapter, we will explore how couples can build a legacy of love through their faith, values, and the example they set for their families and the world.

Section 1: The Impact of a Christian Marriage on Generations

A Christian marriage has the potential to influence not only the lives of the couple but also the lives of their children, grandchildren, and beyond. We will discuss how the values, faith, and love exhibited in your marriage can leave a lasting legacy.

Section 2: Modeling Christ-Like Love

Christian couples are called to model Christ-like love in their marriage. We will explore how demonstrating love, grace, and forgiveness can serve as a powerful example for children and others who witness the relationship.

Section 3: Passing Down Faith and Values

Faith and values are at the core of a Christian marriage. We will discuss how couples can intentionally pass down their faith and values to their children, creating a spiritual legacy that endures.

Section 4: Teaching Resilience and Perseverance

Life is filled with challenges, and Christian marriages are not exempt from difficulties. We will explore how couples can teach their children resilience and perseverance by navigating challenges with faith and love.

Section 5: Leaving a Mark on the World

A Christian marriage has the potential to impact not only the family but also the community and the world. We will discuss how couples can use their love and faith to make a positive difference in the lives of others and leave a mark on the world.

Section 6: Preparing the Next Generation for Christian Marriage

Couples can actively prepare the next generation for Christian marriage by providing guidance, mentorship, and wisdom. We will explore the role of couples in helping young people understand the principles of Christian marriage and build strong, faith-centered relationships.

Conclusion

A Christian marriage is not just a private commitment but a legacy of love that extends to future generations. In this chapter, we've discussed the impact of a Christian marriage on generations, modeling Christ-like love, passing down faith and values, teaching resilience and perseverance, leaving a mark on the world, and preparing the next generation for Christian marriage. As you continue your journey in Christian marriage, remember that the love and faith you nurture today can leave a lasting legacy of love, grace, and hope for generations to come.

9

Supporting Each Other's Spiritual Growth

In a Christian marriage, spiritual growth is not only a personal journey but also a shared one. This chapter explores the importance of supporting each other's spiritual development, strengthening your bond as a couple and your faith in God.

Section 1: The Role of Faith in a Christian Marriage

Faith is a cornerstone of Christian marriage, and it's essential for couples to support each other in their individual journeys of faith. We will discuss how faith strengthens your love and provides guidance for your marriage.

Section 2: Praying Together and for Each Other

Prayer is a powerful tool for nurturing spiritual growth in a Christian marriage. We will explore the benefits of praying together as a couple and praying for each other's spiritual well-being.

Section 3: Studying the Bible as a Couple

The Bible is a source of wisdom and guidance for a Christian marriage. We will discuss the importance of studying the Bible together, reflecting on its teachings, and applying them to your relationship.

Section 4: Encouraging Spiritual Disciplines

Spiritual disciplines, such as meditation, fasting, and solitude, can deepen your relationship with God. We will explore how couples can encourage and engage in these practices to support each other's spiritual growth.

Section 5: Attending Worship and Serving Together

Worship and service are integral parts of the Christian faith. We will discuss how attending church services, engaging in community worship, and serving together can enhance your spiritual growth as a couple.

Section 6: Nurturing Spiritual Conversations

Open and meaningful conversations about faith and spirituality are crucial for a Christian marriage. We will explore the art of nurturing spiritual discussions that allow you to share your beliefs, questions, and experiences.

Conclusion

Supporting each other's spiritual growth is a vital aspect of a Christian marriage. It not only deepens your personal relationship with God but also strengthens your bond as a couple. In this chapter, we've discussed the role of faith, praying together, studying the Bible, encouraging spiritual disciplines, attending worship, nurturing spiritual conversations, and how these practices can support each other's spiritual growth. As you continue your journey in Christian marriage, remember that a strong faith foundation can help you walk in love and unity, drawing strength from God and each other.

10

Cherishing and Celebrating Your Love

In a Christian marriage, it's essential to cherish and celebrate the love you share. This chapter explores the significance of appreciating your relationship, expressing love, and creating meaningful moments that strengthen the bond between husband and wife.

Section 1: The Beauty of Gratitude in Marriage

Gratitude is a powerful force that can deepen love and connection in a Christian marriage. We will discuss how practicing gratitude can enhance your appreciation of your spouse and your relationship.

Section 2: Expressing Love Through Acts of Kindness

Small acts of kindness can go a long way in expressing love. We will explore how gestures of love and kindness can create an atmosphere of love and care within your marriage.

Section 3: Celebrating Milestones and Special Moments

Life is filled with milestones and special moments that deserve celebration.

We will discuss the importance of marking these occasions in your marriage and how they can reinforce your love and commitment.

Section 4: Building Traditions and Memories

Creating traditions and building lasting memories is a way to make your love enduring. We will explore how couples can establish meaningful traditions and make memories that reflect their unique journey together.

Section 5: Rekindling the Romance

Over time, it's common for the spark of romance to dim. We will discuss how couples can rekindle the romance in their marriage through date nights, surprise gestures, and dedicating time to focus on each other.

Section 6: Nurturing a Lifelong Love Story

A Christian marriage is a lifelong love story that continues to evolve. We will conclude this chapter by reflecting on the significance of nurturing your love story through the years, growing together in faith, unity, and love.

Conclusion

Cherishing and celebrating your love is an essential component of a Christian marriage. It is a reminder of the commitment, joy, and beauty that your relationship brings into your lives. In this chapter, we've discussed the beauty of gratitude, acts of kindness, celebrating milestones, building traditions and memories, rekindling the romance, and nurturing a lifelong love story. As you continue your journey in Christian marriage, remember that love is a gift to be celebrated and cherished, a reflection of God's love for His people, and a source of strength and joy in your lives.

11

The Gift of Forgiveness

Forgiveness is a cornerstone of a Christian marriage. In this chapter, we will explore the profound significance of forgiveness, its role in nurturing love, and the principles of extending and receiving forgiveness within your marriage.

Section 1: Understanding Forgiveness in a Christian Marriage

Forgiveness is an essential aspect of Christian love. We will discuss how forgiveness is rooted in the gospel and the sacrificial love of Christ, and why it is crucial in a marriage relationship.

Section 2: Extending Forgiveness to Your Spouse

Forgiving your spouse is an act of love and grace. We will explore the principles of extending forgiveness, the process of letting go of resentment, and the freedom that forgiveness can bring to your marriage.

Section 3: Receiving Forgiveness with Humility

Receiving forgiveness requires humility and a willingness to acknowledge one's mistakes. We will discuss the role of humility in accepting forgiveness and how it can foster a culture of grace and love within the marriage.

Section 4: Forgiveness as a Path to Healing

Forgiveness is not only a way to reconcile but also a path to healing. We will explore how forgiveness can mend wounds, restore trust, and create a stronger, more resilient marriage.

Section 5: Forgiving Repeated Offenses

In a Christian marriage, there may be times when forgiveness is required for repeated offenses. We will discuss how to approach this situation with wisdom, understanding, and a commitment to growth.

Section 6: The Ongoing Practice of Forgiveness

Forgiveness is not a one-time event but an ongoing practice. We will conclude this chapter by emphasizing the importance of continually extending and receiving forgiveness as a way of nurturing your love and unity in your Christian marriage.

Conclusion

Forgiveness is a powerful and transformative force in a Christian marriage. It reflects the love and grace of Christ and is an essential principle for walking in love, faith, and unity. In this chapter, we've discussed the understanding of forgiveness in a Christian marriage, extending forgiveness, receiving forgiveness with humility, forgiveness as a path to healing, forgiving repeated offenses, and the ongoing practice of forgiveness. As you continue your journey in Christian marriage, remember that forgiveness is a gift that can mend, restore, and strengthen your relationship, allowing you to walk hand in hand in the light of God's love.

12

The Joy of Serving Together

Serving together is a central aspect of Christian marriage. This chapter explores the joy and significance of serving God, each other, and the community as a united team within your marriage.

Section 1: Serving God as a Couple

Serving God together is a way to deepen your spiritual connection. We will discuss how couples can engage in acts of worship, prayer, and ministry as a united front, fostering a sense of unity and faith in their marriage.

Section 2: Supporting Each Other's Callings

Each spouse may have unique callings and gifts from God. We will explore how to support and encourage each other in pursuing individual callings, fostering growth, and fulfilling God's purpose.

Section 3: Serving the Community and Others

Christian love extends beyond the marital relationship to the wider community. We will discuss the importance of serving others through acts of kindness, charity, and ministry as a way to express the love and grace of Christ.

Section 4: Teaching and Modeling Service to Children

Serving as a couple is an opportunity to teach your children about the importance of service. We will explore how couples can model a spirit of service and involve their children in acts of kindness and compassion.

Section 5: Finding Joy in Sacrificial Love

Serving often involves sacrifice. We will discuss how finding joy in sacrificial love, inspired by the example of Christ, can enhance your marriage and bring you closer to each other and God.

Section 6: The Impact of Serving on Unity and Love

Serving together has a profound impact on the unity and love within a Christian marriage. We will conclude this chapter by reflecting on the joy and significance of serving God and others as a united team, fostering love, faith, and unity in your marriage.

Conclusion

Serving together is a testament to the love and faith within a Christian marriage. It is a way to express your devotion to God and your commitment to each other, leaving a lasting impact on your relationship and the world. In this chapter, we've discussed serving God as a couple, supporting each other's callings, serving the community and others, teaching and modeling service to children, finding joy in sacrificial love, and the impact of serving on unity and love. As you continue your journey in Christian marriage, remember that serving together is a joyous and fulfilling path that strengthens your love, faith, and unity, allowing you to walk hand in hand in the light of God's love.

Book Summary: "Walking in Love: Christian Marriage Principles"

"Walking in Love: Christian Marriage Principles" is a comprehensive guide that delves into the foundational principles of a Christian marriage. In a world where relationships are often strained, this book provides a beacon of hope, emphasizing the significance of love, faith, unity, and commitment within the sacred covenant of marriage.

The book consists of twelve thoughtfully crafted chapters, each dedicated to a specific aspect of Christian marriage principles. It begins with a strong emphasis on love, highlighting its biblical significance and the qualities that define Christian love, particularly the concept of agape love. The subsequent chapters explore essential facets of a Christian marriage, including trust, unity, communication, conflict resolution, intimacy, and the role of prayer. Each chapter is steeped in biblical wisdom and practical advice, making it accessible and applicable to couples at any stage of their marital journey.

As the book progresses, it delves into the themes of cherishing and celebrating love, supporting each other's spiritual growth, and embracing the power of forgiveness. These chapters highlight the depth of love and faith required to nurture a strong, lasting Christian marriage.

The latter chapters of the book discuss the significance of building a legacy of love and serving together, both within the marital relationship and in the broader community. These chapters emphasize the interconnectedness of love, faith, and service, illuminating the profound impact a Christian marriage can have on the world.

Throughout "Walking in Love," the reader is reminded of the beauty of gratitude, the importance of humility, and the need for a lifetime of commitment. The book underscores the role of faith in Christian marriage and encourages couples to support each other in their spiritual growth, fostering a sense of unity and devotion that strengthens the marital bond.

In summary, "Walking in Love: Christian Marriage Principles" is a powerful and comprehensive guide for couples seeking to build, strengthen, and nurture their Christian marriages. Rooted in biblical principles and filled with practical insights, this book provides a roadmap for a loving, faithful, and enduring marital relationship. It serves as a beacon of hope and a source of inspiration for couples looking to cultivate love, faith, and unity within their Christian marriage, as they journey hand in hand in the light of God's love.

www.ingramcontent.com/pod-product-compliance
Lightning Source LLC
LaVergne TN
LVHW010442070526
838199LV00066B/6158